Emotional Resilience: Building Strength to Overcome Life's Challenges

Summary

1 Understanding Emotional Resilience

1.1 Definition and Core Concepts

Emotional resilience refers to the ability of an individual to adapt to stress and adversity while maintaining mental health and avoiding negative psychological impacts. This concept is foundational in understanding how people can not only survive but also thrive in the face of challenges. Emotional resilience is not an innate trait that one either possesses or lacks, but rather a set of skills and attitudes that can be developed over time.

The core concepts of emotional resilience include self-awareness, mindfulness, self-care, positive relationships, and purposeful engagement. Self-awareness involves recognizing one's emotions and triggers, which is crucial for managing stress proactively. Mindfulness relates to maintaining a moment-by-moment awareness of one's surroundings and internal feelings without judgment. This practice helps individuals stay grounded during turbulent times.

Self-care is another vital aspect, encompassing both physical and emotional health practices that support overall well-being. Engaging in regular physical activity, getting adequate sleep, eating nutritious foods, and participating in relaxing activities are all forms of self-care that bolster resilience by keeping the body and mind strong.

Maintaining positive relationships is also essential for emotional resilience. Social support can provide encouragement and reduce feelings of isolation during difficult periods. These relationships offer practical help as well as emotional comfort, enhancing one's ability to cope with stress.

Lastly, purposeful engagement involves having goals or activities that provide meaning beyond oneself—whether through professional work, hobbies, or volunteering. This sense of purpose can motivate individuals to persevere through obstacles because they feel connected to something larger than themselves.

In summary, emotional resilience is a multifaceted skill set that enables individuals to navigate life's challenges effectively. By understanding its core concepts—self-awareness, mindfulness, self-care, positive relationships, and purposeful engagement—people can learn strategies to enhance their capacity for resilience. This proactive approach not only helps in coping with current adversities but also prepares individuals for future challenges.

1.2 Psychological Foundations of Resilience

The psychological foundations of resilience are rooted in the interplay between an individual's emotional and cognitive processes. Understanding these foundations is crucial for developing strategies that enhance resilience in the face of adversity. This section explores key psychological theories and mechanisms that underpin resilience, offering deeper insights into how individuals can foster this vital capacity.

At the core of psychological resilience is the concept of **cognitive flexibility**. This refers to the ability to adaptively shift thinking in response to new information or changing circumstances. Cognitive flexibility enables individuals to reframe negative experiences, view challenges from multiple perspectives, and find meaningful solutions in difficult situations. Research suggests that those with higher levels of cognitive flexibility tend to exhibit greater resilience by effectively navigating through life's ups and downs.

Another fundamental aspect is **emotional regulation**, which involves managing one's emotions in a healthy way. Emotional regulation skills allow individuals to experience their emotions without becoming overwhelmed by them, enabling a more measured response to stressors. Techniques such as deep breathing, mindfulness meditation, and progressive muscle relaxation are effective ways to enhance emotional regulation and thus contribute to resilience.

Self-efficacy, or the belief in one's ability to influence events and achieve goals, plays a pivotal role in resilience. High self-efficacy helps individuals persist in their efforts despite setbacks and maintain a proactive approach towards problem-solving. It fosters a sense of control over one's environment, which is essential for maintaining motivation and optimism during challenging times.

Social connections also form an integral part of the psychological foundations of resilience. Positive relationships provide emotional support, practical help, and valuable feedback that can buffer against psychological distress. The presence of supportive social networks enhances an individual's capacity to cope with stress and recover from adverse events more quickly.

In conclusion, the psychological foundations of resilience encompass a blend of cognitive flexibility, emotional regulation, self-efficacy, and social connectivity. By strengthening these areas through targeted interventions and personal practice, individuals can enhance their ability to withstand life's challenges effectively.

1.3 Variability in Natural Resilience Among Individuals

The concept of resilience, while universally applicable, manifests uniquely across different individuals. This variability is influenced by a complex interplay of genetic, psychological, and environmental factors that shape how one responds to stress and adversity. Understanding these differences is crucial for developing personalized strategies to enhance resilience.

Genetic predispositions play a significant role in determining natural resilience. Research indicates that certain genes can affect neurotransmitter systems which influence emotional regulation and stress response. For instance, variations in the serotonin transporter gene have been linked to how effectively individuals can handle stress. However, genetics alone do not dictate resilience outcomes; they interact dynamically with one's environment.

Psychological traits also contribute significantly to resilience variability. Traits such as optimism, flexibility, and the ability to maintain a positive outlook in face of challenges are more prevalent in some individuals than others. These traits enable them to recover from setbacks more quickly and efficiently. Cognitive flexibility, as discussed earlier, allows for adaptive thinking and problem-solving strategies which are critical during stressful situations.

Environmental factors encompass the support systems available to an individual, including family stability, social connections, and access to professional help. A supportive environment can amplify natural resilience by providing resources and emotional support needed during tough times. Conversely, those who face chronic stressors such as ongoing family conflict or community violence may have their resilience eroded over time.

The interaction between these factors illustrates why some individuals bounce back from hardships more readily than others. For example, two people with similar genetic makeup might exhibit different levels of resilience based on their psychological traits and environmental contexts. This underscores the importance of a holistic approach when looking at resilience—not just focusing on inherent traits but also considering the broader context in which an individual operates.

In conclusion, understanding the variability in natural resilience among individuals requires a comprehensive view that considers genetic dispositions, psychological characteristics, and environmental contexts. By acknowledging these diverse influences, we can better support each person's unique journey towards building and maintaining resilience.

2 The Science Behind Resilience

2.1 Biological Aspects of Resilience

The concept of resilience extends beyond psychological boundaries, embedding itself deeply within our biological framework. This section explores the intricate biological mechanisms that underpin resilience, offering insights into how our bodies and brains physiologically support our ability to adapt and thrive in the face of adversity.

At the core of biological resilience are the neurobiological processes that govern our stress responses. The hypothalamic-pituitary-adrenal (HPA) axis plays a crucial role here, regulating the secretion of cortisol, known as the stress hormone. In resilient individuals, the HPA axis exhibits a more adaptive functionality, efficiently managing and terminating the stress response. Research suggests that a well-regulated HPA axis is indicative of better stress recovery and reduced risk of chronic stress-related ailments.

Genetics also play a significant role in determining an individual's capacity for resilience. Certain genetic variants can influence neurotransmitter systems such as serotonin and dopamine, which are critical in mood regulation and motivation, respectively. For instance, variations in the serotonin transporter gene (5-HTT) can affect how individuals respond to stress and trauma, potentially predisposing them to psychological resilience or vulnerability.

Neuroplasticity is another vital component of biological resilience. This refers to the brain's ability to reorganize itself by forming new neural connections throughout life. Neuroplasticity allows us to learn from experiences and adaptively respond to new challenges. Studies have shown that increased neuroplasticity is associated with greater emotional resilience, as it enhances one's ability to cope with future stresses.

Furthermore, immune system functioning has been linked with how effectively we can handle stress and recover from illness or injury. Chronic stress can suppress immune function, while a robust immune response tends to correlate with higher levels of resilience. This relationship highlights how integral physical health is to maintaining psychological well-being under pressure.

In conclusion, understanding these biological foundations not only enriches our comprehension of resilience but also underscores potential interventions that could enhance this quality in individuals who may be more biologically susceptible to adverse effects of stress

2.2 The Role of Neuroplasticity in Emotional Strength

The concept of neuroplasticity is pivotal in understanding how individuals can enhance their emotional resilience. This dynamic quality of the brain to rewire and adapt itself forms the basis for developing greater emotional strength, particularly when faced with stress or adversity.

Neuroplasticity involves the brain's ability to form new neural connections in response to learning or experience. This capability is not static but can be enhanced through various practices such as mindfulness, meditation, and cognitive behavioral therapy (CBT). These activities stimulate the brain's plasticity by encouraging new thought patterns and behaviors, which can lead to improved emotional regulation and resilience.

Research has shown that consistent engagement in these practices can lead to structural changes in the brain. For instance, areas like the prefrontal cortex, which is involved in managing higher-order cognitive functions such as planning, decision-making, and emotional regulation, become more robust. Similarly, the amygdala, which plays a role in processing emotions such as fear and anxiety, shows reduced activity over time with regular mindfulness practice. This suggests a direct link between neuroplasticity and an individual's ability to manage emotional responses effectively.

Moreover, neuroplasticity also supports the 'use it or lose it' theory, implying that neural pathways strengthen through use while unused pathways weaken or are pruned away. This aspect of neuroplasticity means that actively practicing positive emotion regulation strategies can enhance one's capacity for resilience by solidifying beneficial neural pathways.

In addition to psychological interventions, physical exercise is another potent enhancer of neuroplasticity. Regular physical activity increases blood flow to the brain and promotes the growth of new neuronal connections. It also stimulates the production of neurotrophic factors such as Brain-Derived Neurotrophic Factor (BDNF), which supports survival of existing neurons and encourages growth and differentiation of new neurons and synapses.

In conclusion, leveraging neuroplasticity through targeted practices offers a promising avenue for bolstering emotional strength. By continuously engaging in activities that promote brain flexibility and growth, individuals can build a foundation for sustained mental health and resilience against life's challenges.

2.3 Psychological Theories Supporting Resilience

Understanding resilience from a psychological perspective involves exploring various theories that explain how individuals adapt to stress and adversity. These theories not only provide insights into the mechanisms behind resilience but also guide interventions aimed at enhancing this crucial trait.

One foundational theory is the **Biopsychosocial Model**, which posits that resilience results from the interaction between biological, psychological, and social factors. This model suggests that no single factor can fully explain resilience; rather, it is the interplay of an individual's genetic makeup, personal coping strategies, and external support systems. For instance, having a supportive family environment (social) can enhance the effects of positive personal traits such as optimism (psychological) and good physical health (biological).

Another significant theory is **Cognitive Behavioral Theory (CBT)**. CBT asserts that an individual's thoughts and perceptions about adversity significantly influence their ability to cope with stress. By reframing negative thoughts into more positive, realistic ones, people can improve their emotional response to stressors, thereby boosting their resilience. This aligns closely with neuroplasticity concepts where cognitive efforts can lead to tangible changes in brain pathways associated with stress and emotion regulation.

The concept of **Emotional Regulation**, derived from Gross's process model of emotion regulation, is also pivotal in understanding resilience. It emphasizes the processes by which individuals influence which emotions they have, when they have them, and how they experience and express these emotions. Techniques such as cognitive reappraisal or suppression are used to manage emotional responses adaptively—key components in resilient behaviors.

Positive Psychology, introduced by Seligman and Csikszentmihalyi, shifts focus from pathology to optimal human functioning. It explores how qualities like hope, gratitude, and compassion contribute to resilience by fostering a mindset geared towards growth and recovery rather than despair.

In conclusion, these psychological theories collectively underscore the complexity of resilience as a multifaceted construct influenced by a myriad of internal processes and external interactions. Understanding these theories helps in crafting targeted interventions that enhance an individual's capacity to thrive despite challenges.

3 Assessing Personal Resilience Levels

3.1 Tools and Techniques for Measuring Resilience

In the quest to understand and enhance personal resilience, it is crucial to have reliable methods for measuring this quality. Various tools and techniques have been developed to assess resilience, each offering insights into how individuals can withstand and recover from challenges. This section explores some of the most widely used instruments in this field, their applications, and their importance in personal development.

The **Resilience Scale**, originally developed by Wagnild and Young, is a questionnaire that measures individual resilience levels based on five core characteristics: perseverance, equanimity, meaningfulness, self-reliance, and existential aloneness. This scale has been extensively validated and is used in various settings, from clinical psychology to workplace environments, helping individuals understand their capacity to cope with stress.

Another significant tool is the **Connor-Davidson Resilience Scale (CD-RISC)**. It includes 25 items that cover aspects such as adaptability, tolerance of negative affect, and the ability to strengthen through stressors. The CD-RISC is notable for its application across different demographic groups and cultures, making it a versatile tool for global studies on resilience.

In addition to standardized tests, innovative approaches like narrative-based evaluations are gaining traction. These involve analyzing personal stories of adversity and recovery to identify patterns of resilient behaviors. Such qualitative data can complement quantitative scores from scales like the Resilience Scale or CD-RISC, providing a more holistic view of an individual's resilience.

Psychological resilience tests, which often include scenario-based assessments to observe responses to hypothetical stressors.

Behavioral observations, where psychologists or trained professionals evaluate an individual's response to controlled environment challenges.

Biofeedback mechanisms, such as heart rate variability monitoring, which can indicate physiological resilience by measuring how well the body manages stress.

Understanding these tools not only helps individuals recognize their own strengths and areas for improvement but also equips professionals with the means to support their clients effectively. As research continues to evolve in this area, these tools are refined further enhancing our understanding of resilience as a dynamic trait that can be developed over time.

This exploration into tools and techniques for measuring resilience underscores its pivotal role in personal development. By regularly assessing resilience levels using these methods, individuals can strategically navigate life's adversities with greater efficacy and emotional strength.

3.2 Interpreting Your Resilience Score

Once you have completed a resilience assessment using tools like the Resilience Scale or the Connor-Davidson Resilience Scale (CD-RISC), the next crucial step is to interpret your score effectively. Understanding what your resilience score indicates can provide profound insights into your psychological fortitude and areas where there may be room for improvement.

Your resilience score typically reflects how well you can cope with stress, adapt to change, and recover from adversity. High scores generally suggest a strong ability to withstand stressors without significant disruption to one's mental health or daily functioning. On the other hand, lower scores might indicate areas where you could benefit from targeted strategies to enhance your resilience.

Interpreting these scores involves more than just ranking yourself against a scale; it requires a deep dive into specific aspects of resilience that you excel in or need to develop. For instance, if your score on the CD-RISC's adaptability dimension is low, this might suggest that you find it challenging to adjust to new situations or bounce back from setbacks quickly. Recognizing such specifics can guide personal development efforts and help in seeking appropriate support or training.

Moreover, it is essential to consider contextual factors when interpreting your resilience score. Factors such as recent life events, ongoing challenges, and even cultural background can significantly influence how you respond to the questionnaire and thus your scores. For example, someone going through major life changes like a career shift or loss of a loved one might temporarily exhibit lower resilience levels.

To gain a comprehensive understanding of your resilience level, compare qualitative data—such as personal experiences of overcoming adversity—with quantitative scores from assessments. This holistic approach not only validates the numerical score but also enriches the interpretation by linking it with real-life contexts.

In conclusion, interpreting your resilience score is not an endpoint but a starting point for self-awareness and growth. It offers valuable clues about where you stand in terms of emotional and psychological strength and provides direction for enhancing those skills that foster greater resilience over time.

3.3 Identifying Areas for Improvement

After interpreting your resilience score, the next critical step is identifying specific areas where you can enhance your resilience capabilities. This process involves a detailed analysis of each dimension within your resilience assessment, pinpointing weaknesses and strategizing on how to address them effectively.

Firstly, examine the dimensions where your scores were relatively low compared to others. For instance, if adaptability or stress tolerance scored lower, these are indicators that you might struggle with change or managing stress effectively. It's essential to delve into the underlying reasons—whether they stem from past experiences, lack of certain skills, or even prevailing circumstances that might be influencing your ability to cope.

Secondly, consider seeking feedback from peers or mentors who can provide an external perspective on your resilience traits. Sometimes, self-assessments can be biased or incomplete; external observations can highlight blind spots you might not be aware of. This feedback can be particularly insightful when aligned with specific instances where resilience was either demonstrated or lacked.

Thirdly, it's beneficial to reflect on recent challenges and how you responded to them. Analyzing real-life situations helps in understanding practical implications of theoretical resilience levels. Did you recover quickly from setbacks? Were you able to maintain a positive outlook during difficult times? Answers to such questions provide concrete examples of areas needing improvement.

In addition to personal reflection and external feedback, professional development programs focusing on emotional intelligence, stress management techniques, and adaptive thinking can be valuable. These programs offer structured learning and practical exercises designed to strengthen the very skills that underpin resilience.

Finally, integrating regular self-review sessions as part of your ongoing personal development plan ensures continuous improvement. Setting specific goals based on identified weaknesses and tracking progress over time not only enhances resilience but also contributes significantly towards overall personal growth and well-being.

In conclusion, identifying areas for improvement in resilience involves a combination of self-assessment, soliciting external feedback, reflecting on real-life challenges, engaging in targeted learning activities, and maintaining an iterative review process. Each step is crucial in developing a robust action plan tailored to bolstering psychological fortitude across various facets of life.

Strategies for Building Emotional Resilienc

4.1 Developing Mindfulness Practices

Mindfulness, a practice rooted in ancient traditions, has gained modern relevance as a foundational tool for enhancing emotional resilience. It involves cultivating a state of active, open attention to the present moment and can significantly alter how one responds to stress and adversity. By developing mindfulness practices, individuals can learn to observe their thoughts and feelings without judgment, fostering a greater sense of calm and clarity in challenging situations.

The first step in establishing a mindfulness routine is engaging in regular meditation sessions. Meditation helps stabilize the mind and reduces tendencies towards reactive emotional responses. Beginners might start with guided meditations available through apps or online platforms which provide structured pathways to mindfulness. Consistency is key—setting aside even just a few minutes daily for meditation can build mental resilience over time.

Beyond meditation, mindfulness can be integrated into daily activities through mindful eating, walking, or even listening. For instance, mindful eating involves paying full attention to the experience of eating—observing the taste, texture, and sensations of food, which enhances dietary enjoyment and can prevent overeating. Similarly, mindful walking encourages an awareness of each step and breath while moving, connecting the individual more deeply with their environment.

Journaling is another effective technique that complements mindfulness practices by providing a space for reflecting on experiences and emotions in a structured manner. Writing about daily events from a mindful perspective helps solidify the day's lessons and insights gained through other mindfulness exercises.

To deepen one's understanding and commitment to mindfulness, attending workshops or retreats can be beneficial. These programs often offer immersive experiences that help solidify mindfulness skills under the guidance of experienced practitioners. They also provide community support which is crucial in maintaining motivation and deepening practice.

Incorporating these practices into everyday life not only builds emotional resilience but also improves overall well-being by reducing stress levels and enhancing personal joy and satisfaction. As individuals become more adept at observing their internal landscapes without criticism or avoidance, they develop stronger defenses against life's inevitable stresses.

4.2 Enhancing Problem-Solving Skills

Enhancing problem-solving skills is pivotal in building emotional resilience, as it equips individuals with the ability to confront and manage challenges effectively. This skill set not only aids in navigating personal and professional hurdles but also fosters a proactive approach to overcoming adversity.

One fundamental aspect of enhancing problem-solving skills is the development of critical thinking. Critical thinking involves analyzing situations objectively, questioning assumptions, and considering various outcomes before making decisions. This can be practiced through regular reflection on daily decisions or through structured critical thinking exercises that challenge one's usual patterns of thought.

Another key component is creative problem solving, which encourages looking beyond conventional solutions and considering innovative alternatives. Techniques such as brainstorming sessions or mind mapping can stimulate creative thought processes and lead to unique solutions that might not be immediately apparent. Engaging in activities that diverge from routine work, such as arts or crafts, can also enhance one's ability to think outside the box.

Effective communication plays a crucial role in problem-solving as well. It involves clearly articulating problems and proposed solutions to others, as well as actively listening to feedback and alternative perspectives. This can be improved through group activities that require collaborative problem-solving efforts, where team members must communicate effectively to achieve a common goal.

To systematically enhance these skills, setting up simulated problem-solving scenarios can be beneficial. These simulations should involve real-world problems that require a combination of critical thinking, creativity, and communication to resolve. Reflecting on the process post-simulation helps identify strengths and areas for improvement in one's problem-solving approach.

Incorporating these practices into everyday life not only sharpens one's ability to deal with immediate problems but also builds a robust foundation for long-term emotional resilience. As individuals become more adept at handling challenges through enhanced problem-solving skills, they experience reduced stress levels and an increased sense of control over their lives.

4.3 Cultivating a Positive Outlook

Cultivating a positive outlook is essential for building emotional resilience, as it influences how individuals perceive and react to stressors in their environment. This section explores the mechanisms through which a positive outlook can be developed and maintained, even in challenging circumstances.

A positive outlook begins with the practice of gratitude. Regularly acknowledging what one is thankful for has been shown to shift attention away from negative or stressful experiences and towards what is going well. Keeping a gratitude journal or sharing what you are grateful for during family meals can reinforce this habit.

Optimism is another cornerstone of a positive outlook. It involves expecting good things to happen in the future. While some may naturally lean towards optimism, others can cultivate it by consciously challenging pessimistic thoughts or catastrophic predictions about the future with more balanced, realistic assessments. Techniques such as cognitive restructuring, where negative thoughts are systematically challenged and replaced with more positive or realistic ones, can be particularly effective.

Mindfulness also plays a crucial role in cultivating a positive outlook. By staying present and fully engaging with the current moment without judgment, individuals can often circumvent the downward spiral of negativity that accompanies ruminating on past events or worrying about the future. Mindfulness can be practiced through meditation, but also through simple daily activities like mindful eating or walking.

Building strong social connections is vital for maintaining positivity as well. Relationships provide emotional support, which can buffer against stress and help maintain an optimistic view during tough times. Engaging regularly with friends, family, and community groups creates a network of support that reinforces positive feelings and helps keep challenges in perspective.

Finally, setting achievable goals contributes to a positive outlook by providing clear direction and a sense of purpose. Goals give structure to daily life and offer motivation to move forward even when obstacles arise. They should be specific, measurable, attainable, relevant, and time-bound (SMART), ensuring they foster both immediate satisfaction and long-term resilience.

Incorporating these practices into everyday life not only fosters an enduring sense of well-being but also equips individuals with tools to face adversity head-on while maintaining an optimistic stance toward life's challenges.

Practical Applications of Resilience Strategi

5.1 Emotional Resilience in Professional Settings

In the realm of professional development, emotional resilience stands as a cornerstone skill that enables individuals to manage stress, adapt to change, and overcome challenges effectively. This section explores how professionals across various industries can cultivate resilience to enhance their performance and well-being in the workplace.

Emotional resilience in professional settings begins with self-awareness. Understanding one's emotional responses to different situations allows individuals to anticipate triggers and prepare more adaptive responses. For instance, a manager aware of their stress points during high-stake projects can adopt proactive measures such as delegation or mindfulness practices to maintain composure and decision-making clarity.

Communication also plays a critical role in building resilience at work. Transparent communication can create an environment of trust and support among team members. When employees feel secure in expressing their concerns and challenges without fear of judgment, they are more likely to seek help and resources needed to navigate difficult periods. This supportive network acts as a buffer against potential stressors, thereby fostering a resilient organizational culture.

Moreover, developing problem-solving skills is essential for enhancing emotional resilience. Professionals who can approach problems with a flexible mindset are better equipped at finding solutions under pressure, turning obstacles into opportunities for learning and growth. Training sessions that focus on creative problem-solving techniques can equip teams with the tools necessary to thrive in dynamic business environments.

To further reinforce resilience, it is crucial for organizations to encourage continuous learning and development. Providing employees with opportunities to gain new skills or advance their knowledge not only boosts their confidence but also prepares them for unforeseen challenges ahead. Additionally, leaders who promote a growth mindset by recognizing efforts and learning from failures contribute significantly to building resilient teams.

In conclusion, cultivating emotional resilience in professional settings involves a multifaceted approach centered around self-awareness, effective communication, adept problem-solving, and continuous personal growth. By integrating these strategies into daily operations, businesses can create robust workforces capable of succeeding in today's ever-evolving corporate landscape.

5.2 During Personal Life Challenges

Personal life challenges often test our emotional resilience in profound ways, pushing us to adapt and thrive amidst adversity. This section delves into the strategies that individuals can employ to maintain resilience during personal crises such as loss, illness, or significant life changes.

Firstly, acknowledging and accepting one's emotions plays a pivotal role in building resilience. Unlike professional settings where emotional responses might be subdued for the sake of decorum, personal challenges require us to confront our feelings directly. Engaging with these emotions through therapy, journaling, or conversations with trusted friends can provide a release and foster a deeper understanding of oneself.

Moreover, maintaining a support network is crucial during tough times. This network may include family members, close friends, or community groups who provide emotional comfort and practical help. Unlike in professional environments where support might focus on task-related assistance or career advice, personal support systems offer empathy and understanding which are vital for emotional recovery and resilience.

Adapting healthy coping mechanisms also forms an essential part of dealing with personal life challenges. Activities such as mindfulness meditation, regular physical exercise, or engaging in hobbies not only help distract the mind from current stresses but also contribute to long-term emotional well-being. These activities encourage a sense of normalcy and control amidst chaos.

In addition to individual efforts, seeking professional help from counselors or therapists can be beneficial. Professionals can offer strategies and tools tailored to one's specific needs that might not be available through personal research or informal advice. They provide a structured approach to overcoming personal obstacles and enhancing resilience.

Last but not least, setting realistic goals and celebrating small achievements can significantly boost morale and encourage persistence during difficult periods. Whether it's returning to daily routines after a loss or gradually overcoming a health challenge, recognizing each step forward can reinforce a sense of progress and capability.

In conclusion, while both professional and personal settings demand emotional resilience, the approaches in personal scenarios are deeply intertwined with genuine self-care practices and the support of loved ones. By embracing these strategies, individuals can navigate their toughest times with strength and grace.

5.3 In Academic and Learning Environments

In the context of academic and learning environments, resilience strategies play a crucial role in helping students navigate the myriad challenges that come with pursuing education. This section explores how resilience can be fostered among students to enhance their educational outcomes and overall well-being.

One fundamental aspect of building resilience in educational settings is the development of a supportive learning environment. Educators and administrators can create this by promoting an inclusive atmosphere that respects diverse backgrounds and learning styles. For instance, implementing policies that address and prevent bullying helps in creating a safe space for all students, which is essential for their emotional security and academic performance.

Moreover, integrating social-emotional learning (SEL) into the curriculum is another effective strategy. SEL programs are designed to teach students skills such as empathy, self-regulation, and collaboration. These skills not only help students manage their emotions and build healthy relationships but also equip them to handle academic pressures better. For example, teaching students about mindfulness techniques can reduce anxiety before tests and improve focus during classwork.

Resilience in academic settings also involves teaching students how to cope with failures and setbacks effectively. This can be achieved through constructive feedback mechanisms where failures are seen as opportunities for learning rather than just negative outcomes. Educators can encourage this perspective by sharing their own experiences with failure as part of the learning process, thereby normalizing it and reducing the stigma associated with making mistakes.

Additionally, fostering strong relationships between teachers and students is vital for resilience. When students feel they have mentors who believe in their capabilities, they are more likely to persevere through difficulties. Teachers can nurture these relationships by being accessible and attentive to individual student needs, thus providing personalized support that fosters an empowering learning environment.

In conclusion, academic resilience is not merely about encouraging hard work; it's about cultivating an educational ecosystem that promotes emotional intelligence, supports risk-taking in learning without fear of failure, and champions interpersonal connections among school community members. By embedding these principles into everyday educational practices, institutions can significantly enhance student resilience leading to improved educational achievements and personal growth.

6 Case Studies on Emotional Resilience

6.1 Overcoming Personal Loss

Personal loss is an inevitable part of life, yet its impact can shake the very foundation of our emotional and psychological well-being. Overcoming such losses requires more than time; it demands active engagement with one's grief and emotions. This section explores the journey through personal loss, emphasizing strategies that foster emotional resilience and facilitate healing.

The first step in navigating personal loss is acknowledging the pain. Suppressing grief can lead to prolonged sorrow or complicated grief disorders. It is crucial for individuals to allow themselves to experience their feelings without judgment. This process involves understanding that grief does not follow a linear path and that fluctuations in emotions are normal.

Building a support system plays a vital role in overcoming personal loss. Connecting with friends, family, or support groups provides emotional comfort and practical help during difficult times. Sharing one's feelings with others who have experienced similar losses can also offer insights and coping mechanisms that might not be apparent when dealing with grief alone.

In addition to social support, engaging in self-care activities is essential for maintaining physical and mental health during the grieving process. This might include regular exercise, adequate sleep, nutritious eating, and mindfulness practices such as meditation or yoga. These activities help stabilize mood swings and combat depression, making it easier to manage daily tasks and responsibilities.

Another effective strategy is finding meaning after loss through activities such as volunteering, creative arts, or spiritual practices. Such engagements do not diminish the sense of loss but can help individuals construct a new sense of purpose that incorporates their experiences of grief into a broader context of personal growth and resilience.

Lastly, professional help from psychologists or counselors should be considered when grief feels unmanageable. Therapy can provide structured ways to understand and work through complex emotions that arise after significant losses.

Overcoming personal loss is not about moving on from the memory of loved ones but rather integrating this memory into ongoing life experiences in a way that honors the past while embracing the future. By actively cultivating resilience through these strategies, individuals can navigate their journey through grief with strength and grace.

6.2 Handling Failure and Setbacks

Failure and setbacks are universal experiences that test our emotional resilience, yet they also provide powerful opportunities for growth and learning. Understanding how to effectively handle these challenges is crucial for personal development and long-term success.

The initial step in managing failure is the acceptance of the situation. Recognizing that setbacks are not reflections of one's worth but rather part of the human experience can alleviate some of the emotional burden. This mindset shift is essential as it lays the foundation for constructive analysis and forward movement.

Once acceptance is established, reflection becomes a key process. It involves analyzing what went wrong and why, without dwelling on it excessively. This reflective practice should be objective and focused on extracting lessons that can inform future actions. For instance, a business failure could reveal insights about market dynamics or personal management styles that need adjustment.

Building resilience against future setbacks involves developing a proactive recovery plan. This includes setting new goals based on learned lessons, which helps maintain motivation and direction. Additionally, integrating routine resilience-building practices such as mindfulness, regular physical activity, and maintaining a balanced diet can enhance one's ability to cope with stress and recover from setbacks more efficiently.

Social support also plays a critical role in overcoming failures. Sharing experiences with friends, family, or mentors who offer encouragement and advice can provide emotional relief and practical insights. Moreover, seeing how others have overcome similar obstacles can serve as inspiration and proof that beyond failure lies the possibility of success.

Finally, it's important to cultivate a growth mindset—a belief that abilities can be developed through dedication and hard work. This perspective encourages persistence despite failures because each attempt is seen as a step towards mastering a skill rather than a final judgment of capability.

In conclusion, handling failures effectively requires acceptance, reflection, proactive planning, social support, and cultivating a growth mindset. By embracing these strategies, individuals can transform their setbacks into stepping stones towards success.

6.3 Managing Chronic Stress

Chronic stress is a pervasive issue in modern society, affecting numerous aspects of personal health and well-being. It differs from acute stress in that it is constant and persists over an extended period of time. Managing chronic stress effectively is crucial for maintaining mental, emotional, and physical health.

The first step in managing chronic stress involves identifying its sources. These can range from job insecurity, long-term relationship problems, to ongoing financial worries. Recognizing these triggers allows individuals to address the root causes or find ways to mitigate their impact.

Once the sources are identified, developing coping strategies becomes essential. Techniques such as mindfulness meditation, deep breathing exercises, and yoga have been shown to reduce symptoms of stress by enhancing relaxation and focus. Regular physical activity is another effective method; it not only helps in reducing the levels of the body's stress hormones, such as adrenaline and cortisol but also stimulates the production of endorphins, chemicals in the brain that are natural painkillers and mood elevators.

Nutrition also plays a critical role in how effectively we manage stress. Consuming a balanced diet rich in antioxidants and omega-3 fatty acids can help fortify the body's resilience against the impacts of stress. Avoiding excessive caffeine and sugar intake can prevent the peaks and troughs in energy that exacerbate stress levels.

Sleep is another fundamental element in managing chronic stress effectively. Lack of sleep can exacerbate anxiety and decrease cognitive function, making it harder to deal with daily stresses. Establishing a regular sleep routine that includes 7-9 hours of uninterrupted sleep can significantly improve an individual's ability to cope with prolonged stressful situations.

Finally, seeking social support from friends, family, or professional counselors can provide emotional comfort and practical advice for managing stressors. Sharing one's feelings with others leads to decreased feelings of isolation and increased feelings of being understood and supported.

In conclusion, managing chronic stress requires a comprehensive approach that includes identifying triggers, employing physical and mental relaxation techniques, maintaining proper nutrition and sleep habits, and seeking social support. By integrating these strategies into daily life routines, individuals can enhance their resilience against chronic stressors thereby improving their overall quality of life.

7 Expert Opinions and Insights

7.1 Contributions from Psychology Professionals

In the exploration of emotional resilience, psychology professionals play a pivotal role by providing deep insights into the psychological mechanisms that underpin this crucial trait. Their contributions are instrumental in shaping both theoretical frameworks and practical applications that assist individuals in enhancing their capacity to withstand life's challenges.

One significant contribution from psychology professionals is the identification and explanation of cognitive and emotional aspects of resilience. They delve into how our thoughts, beliefs, and emotions influence our ability to cope with stress and adversity. For instance, cognitive-behavioral approaches are frequently discussed, highlighting how modifying one's thought patterns can lead to better stress management and improved overall well-being.

Moreover, psychologists have contributed extensively to understanding the role of personality traits such as optimism and perseverance in building resilience. Research indicates that these traits can significantly affect how individuals perceive and react to stressors. By fostering an optimistic outlook, individuals can view potential setbacks as opportunities for growth rather than insurmountable obstacles.

Another area where psychology professionals have made substantial contributions is in the development of intervention strategies that promote resilience. These include mindfulness training, which helps individuals maintain focus on the present moment and develop an attitude of acceptance toward life's fluctuations; and resilience training programs designed specifically for workplaces or schools to help people adapt to new challenges while maintaining mental health and productivity.

The integration of real-life case studies into psychological research has also enriched our understanding of resilience. These narratives not only illustrate theoretical concepts but also provide relatable examples of how diverse strategies can be effectively applied in various situations ranging from personal crises to professional setbacks.

Finally, psychology professionals emphasize the importance of social support systems in cultivating resilience. They explore how relationships with family, friends, colleagues, and mentors provide emotional scaffolding that helps individuals navigate through tough times more effectively.

In summary, the contributions from psychology professionals are multifaceted—ranging from theoretical research to practical interventions—and crucial for anyone looking to build or enhance their emotional resilience. Through their work, they offer valuable tools that empower us to thrive even in the face of adversity.

7.2 Insights from Neuroscience Researchers

Neuroscience researchers provide critical insights into the biological foundations of emotional resilience, exploring how brain structures and functions contribute to our ability to manage stress and recover from adversity. This research is pivotal in bridging the gap between psychological theories and physiological realities, offering a more comprehensive understanding of resilience.

One key area of focus is the role of the prefrontal cortex (PFC) and amygdala in emotional regulation. Studies show that the PFC helps modulate responses to stress, with a well-functioning PFC associated with better control over emotional reactions facilitated by the amygdala. This interaction is crucial for maintaining emotional stability and adapting to new or challenging situations effectively.

Neuroscientists also investigate the impact of neuroplasticity on resilience. Neuroplasticity refers to the brain's ability to adapt its structure and function in response to experiences. Research indicates that engaging in activities that promote positive neuroplastic changes—such as mindfulness meditation, physical exercise, and cognitive training—can enhance an individual's resilience by strengthening neural pathways associated with positive emotions and stress reduction.

Another significant contribution from neuroscience is the study of neurotransmitters like serotonin and dopamine, which play roles in mood regulation and motivation, respectively. Understanding how these chemicals influence our feelings and behaviors during stressful times can lead to targeted therapies that boost resilience. For instance, interventions that increase serotonin levels might improve mood stability, thereby enhancing an individual's capacity to cope with stress.

In addition to biochemical studies, neuroimaging technologies such as fMRI have allowed researchers to observe real-time brain activity patterns related to resilience strategies like reappraisal or suppression. These insights help clarify why certain individuals bounce back from setbacks more effectively than others and guide the development of personalized intervention programs.

In conclusion, neuroscience researchers contribute extensively by elucidating the complex neural mechanisms underlying resilience. Their work not only deepens our understanding but also opens avenues for innovative treatments designed to enhance mental fortitude across diverse populations.

The integration of neuroscience findings with psychological practices enriches our approach towards building resilience by providing a biologically informed perspective on intervention strategies. It underscores the importance of a multidisciplinary approach in addressing mental health challenges, ensuring interventions are not only psychologically sound but also biologically attuned.

7.3 Advice from Therapeutic Practitioners

The insights provided by therapeutic practitioners are invaluable in the practical application of theories surrounding emotional resilience and stress management. These professionals, including psychologists, counselors, and therapists, offer a unique perspective that bridges theoretical knowledge with real-world application, enabling individuals to enhance their coping mechanisms in everyday life.

One critical area where therapeutic practitioners contribute is in the personalized adaptation of coping strategies. They work closely with individuals to identify specific stress triggers and develop tailored approaches to manage them. This personalized strategy is crucial because it considers the unique psychological makeup of each person, which can significantly differ due to factors like past trauma, current circumstances, and individual personality traits.

Therapeutic practitioners also emphasize the importance of building a strong therapist-client relationship as a foundation for effective therapy. This relationship fosters trust and openness, allowing clients to share their feelings without judgment, which is essential for addressing deep-seated emotional issues. Techniques such as active listening and empathetic understanding are key tools used by therapists to build this rapport.

In addition to traditional therapy techniques, many practitioners are now incorporating integrative approaches that include mindfulness-based stress reduction (MBSR), cognitive-behavioral therapy (CBT), and other modalities that have been shown to improve mental resilience. For instance, MBSR teaches clients how to remain present in the moment and engage with their thoughts and feelings without judgment—skills that are vital for managing anxiety and reducing overall stress levels.

Furthermore, therapeutic practitioners often advocate for a holistic approach to mental health that includes physical wellness. Regular physical activity, adequate sleep, and proper nutrition are frequently discussed as essential components of maintaining not only physical but also mental health. By integrating these elements into treatment plans, therapists help clients build a comprehensive lifestyle framework that supports sustained emotional well-being.

The advice from therapeutic practitioners thus plays a pivotal role in translating neuroscientific findings into actionable strategies that individuals can use to enhance their resilience against stress. By combining evidence-based practices with compassionate care, they facilitate deeper personal growth and improved mental health outcomes.

Tools and Resources for Enhancing Resilien

8.1 Digital Apps and Online Platforms

In the realm of emotional resilience, digital apps and online platforms have emerged as vital tools that assist individuals in managing stress, enhancing mindfulness, and improving overall mental health. These technological solutions offer accessible resources that can be tailored to meet personal needs, making them an integral part of modern strategies for building resilience.

One significant advantage of these digital tools is their ability to provide immediate support and feedback. Apps like Headspace and Calm offer guided meditations that help users reduce anxiety and increase awareness of their mental state. These platforms are designed with user-friendly interfaces that encourage regular use, which is crucial for developing habits that foster resilience. Moreover, many apps incorporate goal-setting features and progress tracking, empowering users to take control of their emotional growth.

Another key aspect of these platforms is the community support they facilitate. Social features such as forums or group challenges enable users to connect with others facing similar challenges. This sense of community not only provides emotional support but also motivates individuals to engage more deeply with resilience-building activities. For instance, the app Seven Cups connects users with trained listeners to discuss issues confidentially, thereby promoting a supportive network that enhances personal development.

Furthermore, customization options available in these apps play a crucial role in addressing the unique needs of each user. By allowing individuals to tailor activities and notifications based on their personal preferences and goals, apps can become a daily part of one's routine, seamlessly integrating into their lifestyle for ongoing resilience enhancement.

Educational content is another cornerstone of many resilience-focused apps. Platforms like Happify provide science-based activities and games designed to train the brain in positive thinking patterns and coping mechanisms. The integration of expert knowledge helps demystify psychological concepts, making them more accessible to the general public and facilitating a deeper understanding of one's own mental processes.

In conclusion, digital apps and online platforms are transforming the landscape of emotional resilience by making self-help tools widely accessible, fostering supportive communities, providing educational content, and offering customizable experiences tailored to individual needs. As technology continues to evolve, its potential to support mental health and resilience will likely expand even further.

8.2 Books, Workshops, and Seminars

In the journey to enhance personal resilience, books, workshops, and seminars play pivotal roles by providing in-depth knowledge, interactive learning experiences, and direct engagement with experts. These resources serve as essential tools for individuals seeking to deepen their understanding of resilience and apply practical strategies in their daily lives.

Books on resilience cover a wide range of topics from psychological theories to personal memoirs that illustrate resilience in action. Authors like Brené Brown with her book "Daring Greatly" explore the power of vulnerability in building resilience. Such books often provide not only theoretical insights but also practical exercises that readers can implement to foster their own resilience. Additionally, these publications frequently include narratives that resonate with readers, offering them relatable examples of overcoming adversity.

Workshops and seminars offer more personalized and interactive opportunities for learning. These events are typically led by psychologists, life coaches, or experienced practitioners who provide live demonstrations and real-time feedback. Participants benefit from engaging directly with facilitators and peers, which enhances the learning experience through discussions and group activities. For instance, workshops may involve role-playing scenarios that teach participants how to handle stressful situations effectively using resilient behaviors.

Seminars provide a platform for larger audiences and often feature multiple speakers who bring diverse perspectives on resilience. These events can be particularly valuable for networking with others interested in similar topics. The collective environment fosters a sense of community among attendees, reinforcing that the challenges they face are not isolated incidents but common experiences that can be managed with proper support and strategies.

Moreover, many workshops and seminars incorporate case studies or guest speakers who have demonstrated exceptional resilience in their lives or careers. Hearing these stories firsthand not only motivates participants but also provides concrete examples of how the principles of resilience can be applied in various contexts.

In conclusion, books along with workshops and seminars enrich the toolkit available for those aiming to build or enhance their resilience. By combining theoretical knowledge with practical application and peer interaction, these resources create a comprehensive learning environment that supports significant personal development.

8.3 Community Support Networks

Community support networks are vital in fostering resilience among individuals by providing emotional, informational, and practical support. These networks, often formed around shared experiences or common goals, serve as a crucial buffer against the stresses of life's challenges. They operate on various levels—ranging from informal groups to structured organizations—and each plays a unique role in enhancing the collective resilience of its members.

At the grassroots level, community support networks can include neighborhood associations or local groups that organize regular meetings and activities. These gatherings allow members to share their experiences and coping strategies, creating a space where individuals feel understood and supported. For example, a community garden group not only promotes physical activity and environmental responsibility but also fosters social interaction that strengthens community bonds and individual well-being.

Beyond local initiatives, technology has enabled the expansion of support networks through online platforms. Social media groups, forums, and dedicated apps connect individuals from diverse backgrounds but with similar life situations or interests across vast distances. This digital approach to community building provides accessible resources like webinars, shared content such as articles and videos, and real-time communication tools for immediate support.

Furthermore, specialized organizations play a pivotal role in addressing specific needs within a community. For instance, non-profits focusing on mental health might offer workshops that teach resilience-building techniques tailored to those recovering from trauma or dealing with chronic stressors. These programs are often designed with input from psychologists and are facilitated by trained counselors who provide professional guidance.

The effectiveness of these networks often hinges on active participation and mutual respect among members. Successful communities encourage inclusivity and empower individuals to contribute their skills and knowledge, which enhances the sense of ownership and commitment to the group's objectives. Additionally, leadership within these networks is crucial; effective leaders can inspire trust and motivate participation through transparent communication and empathetic governance.

In conclusion, community support networks are indispensable in promoting resilience by offering supportive environments where people can learn from each other's experiences while receiving encouragement during tough times. Whether through face-to-face interactions or virtual connections, these networks provide essential tools for individuals to navigate life's challenges together.

Challenges to Developing Emotional Resilien

9.1 Common Obstacles and How to Overcome Them

Developing emotional resilience is essential for navigating the complexities of modern life, yet several common obstacles can hinder this process. Understanding these barriers and learning effective strategies to overcome them is crucial for anyone looking to enhance their ability to cope with adversity.

Overwhelming Negative Emotions: One of the primary challenges in building emotional resilience is managing intense negative emotions such as fear, anger, or sadness. These emotions can cloud judgment and lead to impulsive actions or withdrawal from challenging situations. To counteract this, individuals can practice mindfulness techniques which help in recognizing these emotions without being overwhelmed by them. Techniques such as deep breathing, meditation, and guided imagery provide a space for calming the mind and gaining perspective.

Persistent Negative Thinking: Another significant barrier is the tendency to engage in negative thinking patterns that reinforce feelings of helplessness and hopelessness. Cognitive-behavioral strategies can be particularly effective here, helping individuals identify and challenge these destructive thoughts. By replacing them with more balanced and constructive thinking, one can gradually shift their mindset towards a more resilient outlook.

Lack of Support Network: Emotional resilience is also impacted by the quality of one's social connections. Isolation can exacerbate stress and hinder coping mechanisms. Building a strong support network—whether through friends, family, or community groups—provides external resources for advice, encouragement, and empathy. Engaging regularly with supportive individuals helps buffer against the effects of stress and provides models for adaptive coping strategies.

Inadequate Self-Care: Neglecting physical health can impair mental health and vice versa; thus, maintaining a routine that includes regular exercise, adequate sleep, and nutritious eating habits is vital. Physical wellness significantly affects psychological well-being and resilience by enhancing mood stability and energy levels.

To effectively build emotional resilience amidst these challenges, it's important to adopt a proactive approach that incorporates self-awareness practices with active seeking of external support when necessary. By understanding personal triggers and responses to stressors—and having strategies in place to manage them—one can navigate through life's adversities with greater ease and confidence.

9.2 Impact of Lifestyle on Resilience

The way individuals live their daily lives plays a crucial role in developing and maintaining emotional resilience. Lifestyle factors such as diet, exercise, sleep, and social interactions directly influence one's ability to cope with stress and rebound from adversity.

Diet and Nutrition: Nutritional choices affect mental health by altering brain structure and function. Foods rich in omega-3 fatty acids, for example, are known to enhance cognitive function and mood stability, which are essential for resilience. Conversely, diets high in refined sugars and unhealthy fats can exacerbate symptoms of depression and anxiety, thereby weakening emotional resilience. Incorporating a balanced diet that includes plenty of fruits, vegetables, lean proteins, and whole grains can help fortify the mind against stress.

Physical Activity: Regular exercise is another pillar of a resilient lifestyle. Physical activity releases endorphins—chemicals in the brain that act as natural painkillers—and improves the ability to sleep, which in turn reduces stress. Moreover, exercise has been shown to mitigate symptoms associated with low self-esteem and social withdrawal through enhanced physical self-perception and opportunities for social interaction.

Sleep Hygiene: Quality sleep is integral to emotional resilience. Sleep deprivation can lead to irritability, increased stress responses, and difficulty concentrating—all of which impair adaptive coping strategies during challenging times. Establishing a regular sleep schedule that includes 7-9 hours of uninterrupted sleep helps maintain the critical balance between bodily systems necessary for optimal emotional response to stress.

Social Connections: The strength of one's social network cannot be overstated when discussing resilience. Engaging regularly with supportive family members or friends provides not only an outlet for sharing feelings but also a source of practical support during difficult periods. Socially connected individuals tend to recover more quickly from setbacks because they have access to emotional comfort and reassurance.

In conclusion, adopting a healthy lifestyle is not merely about physical well-being but is deeply intertwined with mental health and emotional resilience. By managing dietary habits, engaging in regular physical activity, ensuring adequate sleep, and fostering strong social bonds, individuals equip themselves with powerful tools against life's inevitable stresses.

9.3 Cultural Influences on Perceptions of Adversity

Cultural backgrounds significantly shape how individuals perceive and respond to adversity, influencing the development of emotional resilience. This section explores the nuanced ways in which cultural contexts affect interpretations of challenging situations and the strategies employed to cope with them.

In many Western societies, there is a prevalent belief in individualism and self-reliance, which can affect how adversity is perceived. In these cultures, personal achievement and independence are highly valued, and challenges are often seen as opportunities for personal growth. This perspective can encourage a proactive approach to overcoming difficulties but may also lead to pressure to succeed independently without seeking help.

Conversely, in many Eastern cultures, where collectivism is emphasized, adversity might be viewed through a communal lens. The focus here is on interdependence and harmony within the group. Challenges are often approached collectively, and the support of family and community plays a crucial role in coping with stress. This can foster strong social support networks but might also limit personal autonomy in decision-making during crises.

The concept of 'face,' or maintaining social respectability, is another cultural factor that influences responses to adversity, particularly in Asian cultures. The desire to uphold family honor can impact how individuals deal with setbacks—either by motivating resilience to avoid shame or by discouraging open acknowledgment of personal struggles.

In many indigenous cultures, adversity is integrated into a broader spiritual or holistic worldview. Challenges are often seen as an essential part of life's journey or as tests from a higher power. Such perspectives can provide a comforting framework that helps individuals find meaning in their struggles and fosters resilience through spiritual or communal practices.

Understanding these cultural nuances is crucial for developing effective support systems that respect diverse values and coping mechanisms. It highlights the importance of culturally sensitive approaches in psychological interventions and resilience-building programs that cater to the specific needs and beliefs of different communities.

In conclusion, culture profoundly shapes how we interpret challenges and marshal resources to cope with them. Recognizing and integrating cultural contexts into resilience training can enhance its effectiveness by aligning strategies with the values, beliefs, and practices prevalent in each culture.

0 Long-Term Benefits of Emotional Resilien

10.1 Improved Mental Health Outcomes

Emotional resilience, a critical skill in managing life's challenges, plays a pivotal role in shaping mental health outcomes. This section explores how developing resilience contributes to enhanced mental well-being, providing individuals with the tools to handle stress, adversity, and trauma more effectively. The ability to bounce back from setbacks not only prevents various mental health conditions but also promotes overall psychological wellness.

Research indicates that individuals with high levels of emotional resilience exhibit fewer symptoms of common mental health disorders such as anxiety and depression. This is largely due to their capacity to adapt to stressful situations and recover from hardship without long-term negative consequences on their mental health. Resilient individuals tend to maintain a positive outlook and manage emotions in ways that prevent overwhelming stress and burnout.

Moreover, emotional resilience fosters a sense of mastery and control over one's life circumstances, which is crucial for self-esteem and confidence. By viewing challenges as opportunities for growth rather than insurmountable obstacles, resilient people can navigate through life's ups and downs more smoothly. This perspective significantly reduces feelings of helplessness and despair, which are common triggers for mental health issues.

The development of emotional resilience also enhances social relationships, an important aspect of good mental health. Resilient individuals are better equipped to seek support when needed and provide support to others, creating strong networks of social support that buffer against psychological distress. Furthermore, these supportive relationships contribute to a greater sense of belonging and purpose, both of which are vital for emotional well-being.

In conclusion, cultivating emotional resilience is not just about surviving the tough times; it fundamentally enriches one's quality of life by improving mental health outcomes across various dimensions. It empowers individuals with the ability to not only withstand but thrive amidst life's challenges—transforming potential adversities into avenues for personal growth and fulfillment.

10.2 Enhanced Relationship Dynamics

Emotional resilience significantly influences the quality and dynamics of interpersonal relationships. Individuals who possess a high degree of emotional resilience are better equipped to manage conflicts, communicate effectively, and foster deeper connections with others. This section delves into how emotional resilience can enhance relationship dynamics across personal and professional spheres.

Firstly, resilient individuals tend to exhibit greater empathy and understanding towards others' feelings and perspectives. This empathetic approach allows them to navigate social interactions more smoothly, reducing the likelihood of misunderstandings and conflicts. For instance, in a family setting, a parent with high emotional resilience is more likely to handle children's mood swings or disagreements calmly, promoting a nurturing environment that strengthens familial bonds.

In romantic relationships, resilience contributes to stability by enabling partners to bounce back from setbacks or disagreements without harboring resentment or distress. Such couples often use challenges as opportunities for growth, enhancing their mutual understanding and commitment. Moreover, resilient individuals are typically more open to discussing issues openly and seeking solutions collaboratively, which is crucial for maintaining healthy long-term relationships.

Professionally, emotional resilience fosters better teamwork and leadership. Resilient leaders are adept at managing stress and can thus maintain a positive team atmosphere even under pressure. They inspire trust and respect through their ability to cope with uncertainty and change, making them effective role models. Additionally, such leaders are proficient in recognizing the needs of their team members, adapting their management style accordingly to motivate each individual optimally.

The benefits of emotional resilience extend beyond immediate social interactions; they also contribute significantly to building robust networks of support. Resilient individuals tend not only to seek support when needed but also provide substantial support to others. This reciprocal exchange fortifies relationships against potential stressors or crises, creating a supportive community that enhances collective well-being.

In conclusion, developing emotional resilience is crucial not just for individual well-being but also for cultivating healthier, more dynamic relationships across all areas of life. By improving communication skills, empathy levels, conflict resolution abilities, and support mechanisms within relationships, emotionally resilient individuals enjoy more fulfilling interactions and stronger connections with those around them.

10.3 Greater Career Success

Emotional resilience not only enhances personal relationships but also plays a pivotal role in achieving greater career success. Individuals who exhibit high levels of emotional resilience are more likely to thrive in various professional settings due to their ability to adapt to change, handle stress effectively, and recover from setbacks swiftly.

One significant aspect of how emotional resilience contributes to career success is through improved problem-solving skills. Resilient individuals approach challenges with a solution-oriented mindset, often leading to innovative solutions that may go unnoticed by others less equipped to handle pressure. This capability makes them invaluable assets in workplaces that are dynamic and often unpredictable.

Moreover, emotionally resilient professionals tend to have better leadership qualities. They inspire confidence and loyalty among their peers and subordinates by demonstrating control and optimism in the face of difficulties. Such leaders are adept at keeping their teams motivated during tough times, which is crucial for maintaining productivity and morale. Their ability to model resilience can permeate throughout the team, fostering a generally resilient workplace culture.

Another key benefit of emotional resilience in the professional sphere is enhanced communication skills. Resilient individuals communicate clearly and assertively without letting emotions dictate their responses. This clarity helps prevent misunderstandings and builds trust among colleagues, which is essential for effective teamwork and collaboration.

Furthermore, emotionally resilient individuals are typically more persistent and less likely to give up in the face of adversity. Their perseverance often leads them to achieve long-term goals that require sustained effort and dedication—qualities highly prized in any professional field.

In conclusion, developing emotional resilience can significantly impact one's career trajectory by enhancing leadership abilities, problem-solving skills, communication techniques, and overall persistence. These attributes not only help individuals excel in their current roles but also pave the way for upward mobility within their careers, making emotional resilience a critical factor for professional success.

11 Integrating Resilience into Daily Life

11.1 Daily Practices for Maintaining Resilience

Maintaining resilience in the face of life's challenges is not merely about reacting to adversity but proactively building strength through daily practices. These routines are designed to enhance one's capacity to remain flexible, recover quickly from difficulties, and maintain a positive outlook despite the uncertainties of everyday life.

One fundamental practice is the cultivation of mindfulness. Engaging in regular mindfulness exercises such as meditation or mindful breathing helps individuals center their thoughts and emotions, reducing stress and anxiety. This focused state of being allows one to respond more calmly and effectively to unexpected events, thereby enhancing emotional resilience.

Another vital daily practice involves maintaining physical health. Exercise not only strengthens the body but also boosts mental health by releasing endorphins, chemicals in the brain that act as natural painkillers and mood elevators. Regular physical activity, whether it's a brisk walk or a structured workout session, can significantly improve one's mood and ability to cope with stress.

Building strong social connections is also crucial for resilience. Establishing supportive relationships provides a network of assistance during tough times. Daily interactions with friends, family, or colleagues can offer emotional support and practical help when needed. Moreover, helping others can reinforce one's sense of purpose and self-worth, further contributing to resilience.

Journaling is another effective tool for fostering resilience on a daily basis. By regularly writing down thoughts and feelings, individuals can gain insights into their behaviors and patterns that emerge during challenging times. This reflection can lead to better problem-solving strategies and a greater understanding of how to navigate future obstacles more effectively.

Lastly, setting realistic goals each day can give a sense of accomplishment and direction. These goals should be achievable and measurable; they serve as stepping stones towards larger objectives while providing motivation and structure in daily life.

Incorporating these practices into everyday routines does not require monumental changes but rather small consistent efforts that collectively fortify an individual's resilience over time. By engaging in these activities regularly, individuals equip themselves with tools necessary for dealing with life's unpredictabilities effectively.

11.2 Setting Realistic Goals for Growth

Setting realistic goals is a cornerstone of personal and professional development, particularly in the context of building resilience. This process involves not only identifying achievable objectives but also understanding one's current capabilities and limitations. It serves as a bridge between daily practices of resilience and long-term aspirations, ensuring that each step taken is both purposeful and manageable.

The first step in setting realistic goals is self-assessment. This involves a thorough evaluation of one's strengths, weaknesses, resources, and constraints. Understanding these factors helps in formulating goals that are not only challenging but also attainable within a given timeframe. For instance, someone might aim to improve their emotional resilience by practicing mindfulness for ten minutes daily before setting more ambitious targets like attending a meditation retreat.

Another critical aspect is the SMART criteria—goals should be Specific, Measurable, Achievable, Relevant, and Time-bound. Applying this framework ensures clarity and precision in goal-setting which facilitates easier monitoring and adjustment along the way. For example, rather than vaguely aiming to "be more resilient," a more effective goal would be "to read one book per month on resilience or related skills over the next year."

Incremental progression is vital when setting goals for growth. Small successes build confidence and momentum, making larger challenges seem more approachable. This method also allows for regular feedback loops where strategies can be adjusted based on what is or isn't working. Celebrating these small victories can significantly boost morale and encourage persistence.

Lastly, it's important to maintain flexibility in goal-setting to adapt to changing circumstances without losing sight of the overall objective. Life's unpredictability may necessitate goal recalibration from time to time; hence resilience involves staying committed to growth despite these shifts.

In conclusion, integrating realistic goal-setting into daily life fosters sustained growth by aligning short-term actions with long-term objectives while accommodating life's inherent uncertainties. By methodically setting and pursuing well-defined goals, individuals enhance their capacity to navigate through challenges effectively—thereby strengthening their overall resilience.

11.3 Balancing Work, Life, and Emotional Well-Being

The quest for a harmonious balance between work, life, and emotional well-being is pivotal in fostering resilience and sustaining personal growth. This balance is not merely about dividing hours between office and home but involves integrating wellness practices into all facets of life to enhance overall satisfaction and productivity.

Understanding the interplay between these areas begins with recognizing that work-life balance does not imply an equal split of time. Instead, it focuses on achieving optimal functionality where professional responsibilities do not overshadow personal happiness and health. The integration of emotional well-being into this equation is crucial as it underpins one's ability to perform effectively at work and enjoy fulfilling personal relationships.

One effective strategy for maintaining this balance is setting boundaries. Clear demarcations of when work begins and ends can help prevent job responsibilities from spilling over into personal time. Technology, while a facilitator of workplace efficiency, should be managed wisely—notifications can be silenced during family meals or leisure activities to ensure presence in the moment.

Mindfulness practices are another essential component. Regular mindfulness exercises improve focus and reduce stress levels, making it easier to transition between roles at work and home smoothly. For instance, a brief meditation or deep-breathing session before leaving the office can reset one's emotional state and enhance evening interactions with family or friends.

Physical activity should also be incorporated into daily routines as it boosts mental health by reducing symptoms of depression and anxiety while increasing overall energy levels. This could mean choosing stairs over elevators during the workday or scheduling regular walks after dinner.

Last but not least, fostering strong support networks both professionally and personally can provide emotional safety nets that encourage risk-taking in both domains without fear of failure overwhelming one's sense of self-worth. Engaging regularly with mentors, peers, friends, and family who provide encouragement and feedback helps maintain perspective on what truly matters in both career ambitions and personal aspirations.

In conclusion, balancing work, life, and emotional well-being requires conscious effort to integrate wellness practices across all aspects of life. By setting boundaries, practicing mindfulness, staying active physically, and nurturing supportive relationships, individuals can build resilience that enhances their capacity to thrive amidst various challenges.

12 Future Directions in Resilience Researc

12.1 Emerging Trends in Psychological Studies

In the realm of psychological resilience, recent advancements have begun to highlight the dynamic interplay between neurobiology and environmental factors. This emerging trend focuses on how genetic predispositions and brain chemistry interact with personal experiences to shape an individual's capacity for resilience. Researchers are increasingly using neuroimaging technologies to observe real-time brain activity as individuals respond to stress, providing deeper insights into the neural pathways that underpin resilience.

Another significant trend is the exploration of cultural influences on resilience. Studies are expanding beyond Western-centric models to incorporate diverse perspectives and practices from around the world. This includes examining how different cultures teach coping mechanisms and resilience through community support systems, rituals, and traditional wisdom. Such research underscores the importance of context in understanding and fostering resilience, suggesting that what works for one population may not be as effective for another.

The role of technology in building emotional resilience is also gaining attention. Digital tools like apps designed to enhance mindfulness, manage anxiety, or track mood changes are becoming integral parts of interventions aimed at boosting mental health. Virtual reality (VR) is another innovative tool being explored; it immerses individuals in environments where they can practice coping strategies in a controlled yet realistic setting. These technological approaches not only make therapeutic techniques more accessible but also allow users to personalize their journey towards greater emotional strength.

Furthermore, interdisciplinary approaches are enriching our understanding of resilience by integrating insights from psychology, sociology, neuroscience, and even economics. This holistic view facilitates a more comprehensive understanding of how various factors contribute to or hinder resilience building. For instance, economic stability can significantly impact mental health and adaptive capacities, just as psychological well-being can influence economic decisions and opportunities.

These trends indicate a shift towards more personalized and culturally sensitive approaches in studying psychological resilience. By embracing complexity and leveraging new technologies, researchers aim to develop more effective strategies that cater to individual needs while considering broader socio-cultural dynamics.

12.2 Technological Advancements Aiding Resilience Training

The integration of technology into resilience training represents a significant leap forward in psychological health interventions. As digital platforms become more sophisticated, they offer unique opportunities for individuals to engage in resilience-building practices from anywhere in the world. This section explores how various technological advancements are enhancing the effectiveness and accessibility of resilience training.

One of the most promising technologies in this field is Virtual Reality (VR). VR immerses users in simulated environments that mimic real-life stressors or challenges, providing a safe space to practice coping mechanisms. For instance, VR scenarios can be designed to simulate public speaking, social interactions, or even combat situations for military personnel. These immersive experiences allow individuals to gain confidence and mastery over their responses to stressors, which can translate into improved resilience in real-world situations.

Artificial Intelligence (AI) is another frontier enhancing resilience training. AI-driven applications can personalize learning experiences by adapting scenarios based on the user's progress and specific needs. For example, an AI system might analyze a user's reactions during VR sessions and adjust the difficulty level or introduce new coping strategies based on their performance.

This personalized approach helps ensure that the training remains relevant and challenging enough to foster genuine growth.

Wearable technology also plays a crucial role by providing continuous physiological feedback that can be integrated into resilience training programs. Devices like smartwatches and fitness trackers monitor heart rate variability, sleep patterns, and activity levels—key indicators of stress and recovery. By analyzing this data, individuals can learn how their body responds to stress and how effectively they are implementing their resilience strategies over time.

Lastly, mobile applications dedicated to mental health have proliferated, offering tools ranging from mood tracking to mindfulness exercises. These apps make daily resilience practices accessible and trackable, encouraging consistent engagement which is critical for long-term improvement in mental toughness.

In conclusion, technological advancements are significantly transforming the landscape of resilience training by making it more personalized, interactive, and accessible. These innovations not only enhance individual learning experiences but also empower researchers with data-rich insights into the complexities of human resilience.

12.3 Global Perspectives on Building Resilience

The concept of resilience, while universally relevant, manifests differently across global contexts due to cultural, environmental, and socio-economic diversities. This section delves into the various strategies employed worldwide to foster resilience at individual, community, and national levels, highlighting the importance of culturally informed practices.

In Asia, particularly in countries like Japan and South Korea, resilience is often built through community involvement and collective practices. After events such as natural disasters, these societies typically leverage strong community networks that emphasize mutual aid and social cohesion. For instance, after the 2011 earthquake and tsunami in Japan, rebuilding efforts were heavily centered around community consultation and participation which not only restored physical infrastructure but also reinforced social bonds.

In contrast, Western approaches often focus more on individualistic strategies aimed at enhancing personal skills and mental health. In the United States and Europe, there is a significant emphasis on therapy and psychological interventions that encourage personal coping mechanisms for stress management. Programs integrating cognitive-behavioral techniques are common, aiming to empower individuals by improving their personal skill sets.

African nations show a different pattern where resilience is deeply intertwined with cultural heritage and communal identity. In many African communities, resilience practices are embedded within the cultural narratives passed down through generations. These narratives often teach resilience as a communal rather than an individual trait. For example, storytelling sessions that recount past adversities and collective overcoming are common in communities across Sub-Saharan Africa.

Latin America shows a hybrid approach where both community-oriented strategies and individual psychological resilience are promoted. Countries like Brazil have developed unique psycho-social support systems that integrate traditional communal practices with modern psychological theories to address the broad spectrum of challenges faced by diverse populations.

This global overview underscores the necessity of adopting a flexible framework for building resilience—one that is adaptable to different cultural contexts yet grounded in universal principles of human psychology. By understanding these varied approaches, policymakers can better design interventions that are both culturally appropriate and effective in fostering resilience across different populations.

"Emotional Resilience: Building Strength to Overcome Life's Challenges" is a comprehensive guide aimed at helping individuals navigate the complexities of modern life with strength and poise. The book addresses the essential skill of emotional resilience, which is crucial for adapting and thriving amidst life's inevitable adversities. It targets a broad audience, from professionals in high-stress environments to people facing personal difficulties, providing them with practical tools to enhance their resilience.

The structure of the book begins with an exploration of what emotional resilience truly entails, including its psychological underpinnings and the reasons behind varying resilience levels among individuals. This foundational knowledge paves the way for more in-depth discussions on how to actively cultivate resilience through specific practices. Key strategies covered include mindfulness techniques, effective problem-solving skills, and fostering a positive outlook.

Adding depth to the theoretical concepts are real-life examples and case studies that showcase how these resilience strategies can be applied successfully in various challenging situations such as dealing with loss, failure, or chronic stress. Expert opinions interspersed throughout provide scientific validation and additional perspectives on building durability against adversity.

The book emphasizes self-reflection and direct application of its teachings in readers' lives, promoting the idea that while adversity is unavoidable, adopting a resilient mindset can significantly alter one's approach to challenges—transforming potential setbacks into opportunities for personal growth and learning.